INSIGHT FROM TEACHERS
TO KEEP YOU INSPIRED 365 DAYS A YEAR

Teachers Inspiring Teachers

MATTHEW KELLY

BLUE SPARROW
North Palm Beach, Florida

BLUE
sparrow

Design & Illustration by Ashley Wirfel

ISBN: 978-1-63582-185-7 (hardcover)
ISBN: 978-1-63582-219-9 (e-Book)

10   9   8   7   6   5   4   3   2   1

Printed in the United States of America

FIRST EDITION

Table of Contents

Introduction

THERE IS NO national monument for teachers. I have never seen a statue of a teacher. But we all build monuments for teachers in our hearts.

Teachers change our lives. Teachers draw us out of our own tiny little worlds, and give us a broader worldview. They open our hearts and minds to new possibilities.

Everyone has a story about a teacher who changed his or her life. Everyone has a story about a teacher who had a huge impact on his or her life. And people wish they could reconnect with that teacher and thank him or her.

One of the reasons teachers have such a profound impact on our lives is because their work is tired so closely to the meaning and purpose of life. Every parent has the same dream for their child: They want their children to become the-best-version-of-themselves.

Teachers share this dream. At the heart of this gift we call teaching is the very same dream. Great teachers want their students to become the-best-version-of-themselves. In fact, teachers often want it more for their students than their students want it for themselves.

Teaching is a dynamic collaboration. Each teacher works to help each student become all they are capable of becoming.

When you ask people to tell you about the best teacher they ever had, they always seem to articulate two observations. They may not use the same language, but when you get them talking about this teacher who had such an enormous impact on their life, they almost always describe the same two things:

1. She/He helped me become a-better-version-of-myself.
2. He/She was tough but fair.

We love the people in our lives who encourage and challenge us to better ourselves, and we respect forever the leaders in our lives who were tough but fair. Few things endure like respect. We don't respect the teachers who let us get away with anything. We respect the teachers who are tough but fair, but at the same time have our best interests at heart.

I had a science teacher in high school who used to let us do whatever we wanted. At the time we liked that. But we didn't respect him then and we don't respect him now.

Mrs. Miller had taught eighth grade for forty years in a small town in the Midwest. When she retired she spent a lot of time in the rocking chair on her front porch. One day she wondered to herself how much impact she'd had on those young lives.

That afternoon she went grocery shopping. As she made her way down the aisle she heard a voice behind her say, "Is that you, Mrs. Miller?" She turned around and saw a man in his mid-forties and recognized him immediately. It was Jeremy Daniels.

They stood there looking at each other for a moment, and then she said, "Hello, Jeremy."

Jeremy smiled and they began to talk. He explained that he lived in California with his wife and four children, and that he was just back in town for his father's funeral.

"I'm so glad I bumped into you," he continued. "I think of you all the time." Now his eyes began to fill with tears as he said, "Sometimes I wonder what my life would have been like if I hadn't had you in the eighth grade. Before you, I didn't like school. But worse than that, I didn't like learning. You taught me to love learning and I know all of my success is linked to that love of learning."

Now Mrs. Miller's eyes filled with tears. They talked a little more and then Jeremy took her in his arms and hugged her like he would never let her go.

As she drove home, Mrs. Miller knew for sure what she had always suspected: Teachers change lives, and she had mattered to so many students in so many ways she would never know about.

Every day you make sacrifices in order to teach. You sow these sacrifices like seeds, hoping that they will deliver an abundant harvest, not for yourself, but for your students. You have a sense that you are making a difference, but your true impact as a teacher will remain largely unknown.

You will only ever see less than 1 percent of the impact you have as a teacher. Never get discouraged—the good you do as a teacher lives on forever. Your goodness and generosity live on in other people, in other places, and in other times.

Teachers change lives.

Pablo Picasso was walking down the street in Paris one day when a woman recognized and approached him. After introducing herself and praising his work, she asked him if he would consider drawing her portrait and offered to pay him for the piece.

Picasso agreed and sat the woman down on a nearby bench, brought out a sketchbook and pencil, and began to draw her. A small crowd of spectators gathered very quickly, but in less than ten minutes Picasso had finished the drawing. As he handed it to the woman, he said, "That will be five thousand francs."

Surprised at the price, the woman objected, saying, "But Mr. Picasso, it took you only a few minutes." Picasso smiled and replied, "No, my dear woman, you are mistaken. It took me a whole lifetime."

Each time you step into the classroom, you have been preparing to teach that class for your whole life. Your formal studies have prepared you to teach, but so have a thousand other seemingly unrelated events.

The books you read last summer will change the way you teach this year. Forcing yourself to exercise when you would rather not gives you more energy, patience, and focus. The course you took last year will make you a better teacher this year. Taking time for reflection fills you with the courage you need to lead. The people you surround yourself with, and how you let their positivity or negativity influence you, impacts the kind of teacher you are. What you eat, where you go and what you do on vacation, the music you listen to, and the movies you watch all impact you as a teacher.

Thank you for all the little things you do to become a better teacher. These things go unnoticed and you don't get paid for them, but they matter. Thank you for dedicating your life to teaching.

Teachers play an enormous role in society, but you are often underappreciated. Teaching is an exercise in delayed gratification. Children don't fully realize the impact their teachers have had on their lives until decades later. Thank you for your commitment as a professional educator. Teachers change lives. Try to keep that in mind when you get tired or discouraged. You are changing lives.

MATTHEW KELLY

JANUARY 1

"The calling of the teacher . . . There is no craft more privileged. To awaken in another human being powers, dreams beyond one's own; to induce in others a love for that which one loves; to make of one's inward present their future; that is a threefold adventure like no other."

George Steiner

JANUARY 2

"Teaching is an instinctual art, mindful of potential, craving of realizations, a pausing, seamless process."

A. Bartlett Giamatti

JANUARY 3

"When you educate a person, you save a family."

Abhijit Naskar

JANUARY 4

"Teaching is more than imparting knowledge; it is inspiring change. Learning is more than absorbing facts; it is acquiring understanding."

William Arthur Ward

JANUARY 5

"What office is there which involves more responsibility, which requires more qualifications, and which ought, therefore, to be more honorable, than that of teaching?"

Harriet Martineau

JANUARY 6

"I realized if you can change a classroom, you can change a community, and if you change enough communities you can change the world."

Erin Gruwell

JANUARY 7

"Education—whether its object be children or adults, individuals or an entire people, or even oneself—consists in creating motives. To show what is beneficial, what is obligatory, what is good—that is the task of education. Education concerns itself with the motives for effective action. For no action is ever carried out in the absence of motives capable of supplying the indispensable amount of energy for its execution."

Simone Weil

JANUARY 8

"Teaching is the highest art; before the
doctor, there was a teacher."

Steve Perry

JANUARY 9

"Learning is finding out what you already know. Doing is demonstrating that you know it. Teaching is reminding others that they know just as well as you. You are all learners, doers, teachers."

Richard Bach

JANUARY 10

"Education is the most powerful weapon which you can use to change the world."

Nelson Mandela

JANUARY 11

"Learning is more than the acquisition of the ability to think; it is the acquisition of many specialized abilities for thinking about a variety of things."

Lev S. Vygotsky

JANUARY 12

"It goes like this: teaching is touching life."

Jaime Escalante

JANUARY 13

"Our best chance for happiness is education."

Mark Van Doren

JANUARY 14

"The duties of a teacher are neither few nor small, but they elevate the mind and give energy to the character."

Dorothea Dix

JANUARY 15

"Education is the ticket to success."

Jaime Escalante

JANUARY 16

"If you have to put someone on a pedestal, put teachers. They are society's heroes."

Guy Kawasaki

JANUARY 17

"You have to dream. We all have to dream. Dreaming is OK. Imagine me teaching from space, all over the world, touching so many people's lives. That's a teacher's dream! I have a vision of the world as a global village, a world without boundaries. Imagine a history teacher making history!"

Christa McAuliffe

JANUARY 18

"The function of education, therefore, is to teach one to think intensively and to think critically. Intelligence plus character—that is the goal of true education."

Martin Luther King Jr.

JANUARY 19

"Compassion, kindness, empathy, sympathy, mercy, and understanding are six connected values that should be implanted in the young generation, as they are what motivates people to help and stand for each other. A heart that is filled with mercifulness is a heart that will help its society and the whole world to continue, improve, and thrive."

Noora Ahmed Alsuwaidi

JANUARY 20

"The highest purpose of education is to unlearn what we once took for granted, to replace certainty with subtlety, prejudice with compassion, and destiny with possibility."

Neel Burton

JANUARY 21

"Education breeds confidence. Confidence breeds hope. Hope breeds peace."

Confucius

JANUARY 22

"A teacher must busy herself with finding more and more new names to satisfy the insatiable demands of her young charges. This craving which is manifested in their writing is certainly natural. Between the ages of three and five a child's vocabulary grows spontaneously from three hundred to three thousand or more words."

Maria Montessori

JANUARY 23

"The power of education extends beyond the development of skills we need for economic success. It can contribute to nation-building and reconciliation."

Nelson Mandela

JANUARY 24

"Thirty-one chances. Thirty-one futures, our futures. It's an almost psychotic feeling, believing that part of their lives belongs to me. Everything they become, I also become. And everything about me, they helped to create."

Esmé Raji Codell

JANUARY 25

"I gave [my students] a saying : 'I am somebody. I was somebody when I came. I'll be a better somebody when I leave. I am powerful, and I am strong. I deserve the education that I get here.'"

Rita Pierson

JANUARY 26

"Teach what you know, regardless of when you have learned it—teach what you learned yesterday sagely, as if you have known it all your life, and teach what you have known for decades with enthusiasm, as if you learned it only yesterday."

Mercedes Lackey

JANUARY 27

"Participating in the filling of others' brains with knowledge and know-how is just an extraordinary gift only very few have."

Messaoud Mohammed

JANUARY 28

"The purpose of education is to give the body and to the soul all the beauty and all the perfection of which they are capable."

Plato

JANUARY 29

"Some strive to make themselves great. Others help others see and find their own greatness. It's the latter who really enrich the world we live in."

Rasheed Ogunlaru

JANUARY 30

"Success may require many steps. But progress only requires one."

T. Jay Taylor

JANUARY 31

"Children nurtured in kindness learn the value of understanding. Children taught to be self-sufficient, to respect others, to value education and to build life up rather than to tear it down will become adults capable of leading us to a brighter future. For (as Karl Menninger noted) what's done to children, they will do to society."

Steve Goodier

February

FEBRUARY 1

In your teaching show integrity, seriousness, and soundness of speech that cannot be condemned.

Titus 2:8

FEBRUARY 2

"It takes a big heart to help shape little minds."

Anonymous

FEBRUARY 3

"There is no one-size-fits-all in education. Period. What works in my classroom works as well as it does because I feel, with all my heart, that it is the best thing to do."

Stacey Roshan

FEBRUARY 4

"To reach a child's mind, first reach a child's heart."

Edward Mooney, Jr.

FEBRUARY 5

"Teachers have three loves: love of learning, love of learners, and the love of bringing the first two loves together."

Scott Hayden

FEBRUARY 6

"My task as a language arts teacher is to provide texts that are not so difficult that my students shut down in frustration and not so easy that my students don't push their thinking."

Kimberly Hill Campbell

FEBRUARY 7

"We shouldn't teach great books; we should teach a love of reading. Knowing the contents of a few works of literature is a trivial achievement. Being inclined to go on reading is a great achievement."

B. F. Skinner

FEBRUARY 8

"I'm a teacher. A teacher is someone who leads. There is no magic here. I do not walk on water. I do not part the sea. I just love children."

Marva Collins

FEBRUARY 9

"To truly motivate others 1) discover what their motives, desires & drivers are; 2) genuinely connect with and support them from the heart."

Rasheed Ogunlaru

FEBRUARY 10

"When you study great teachers, you will learn much more from their caring and hard work than from their style."

William Glasser

"Teach love, generosity, good manners, and some of that will drift from the classroom to the home and who knows, the children will be educating the parents."

Roger Moore

FEBRUARY 12

"Teaching is an art that can be learned; learning from a teacher is an art that can be learned; anyone who tries—and we all try—can gain a certain competence in teaching; but a real teacher, now—he has a talent. He has a gift like a fine artist or musician or sculptor. Oh, we think highly of teachers, and of teaching. Teaching is part of loving, you know."

Theodore Sturgeon

FEBRUARY 13

"Great teachers emanate out of knowledge, passion and compassion."

A. P. J. Abdul Kalam

FEBRUARY 14

"Multiculturalism compels educators to recognize the narrow boundaries that have shaped the way knowledge is shared in the classroom. It forces us all to recognize our complicity in accepting and perpetuating biases of any kind."

Bell Hooks

FEBRUARY 15

"Educating the mind without educating the heart is no education at all."

Aristotle

FEBRUARY 16

"They may forget what you said but they will not forget how you made them feel."

Carl Buechner

FEBRUARY 17

"A teacher who loves learning earns the right and the ability to help others learn."

Ruth Beechick

FEBRUARY 18

". . . For the object of education is to teach us to love beauty."

Plato

FEBRUARY 19

"Among the many purposes of schooling, four stand out to us as having special moral value: to love and care, to serve, to empower and, of course, to learn."

Andy Hargreaves and Michael Fullan

FEBRUARY 20

"There is no doubt that great teaching and great teachers have a significant impact on students and their long-term association with school and with learning."

Carlos Heleno

FEBRUARY 21

"How do we teach a child—our own, or those in a classroom—to have compassion: to allow people to be different; to understand that like is not equal; to experiment; to laugh; to love; to accept the fact that the most important questions a human being can ask do not have—or need—answers."

Madeleine L'Engle

FEBRUARY 22

"Any genuine teaching will result, if successful, in someone's knowing how to bring about a better condition of things than existed earlier."

John Dewey

FEBRUARY 23

"I never taught language for the purpose of teaching it; but invariably used language as a medium for the communication of thought; thus, the learning of language was coincident with the acquisition of knowledge."

Anne Sullivan Macy

FEBRUARY 24

"Tell me, and I forget. Teach me, and I remember. Involve me, and I learn."

Benjamin Franklin

FEBRUARY 25

"It is essential to understand that battles are primarily won in the heart . . . (people) respond to leadership in a most remarkable way and once you have won (their) heart, (they) will follow you anywhere."

Vince Lombardi

FEBRUARY 26

"Questions are for the benefit of every student, not just the one raising his hand."

Ann Patchett

FEBRUARY 27

"A failure is not always a mistake, it may simply be the best one can do under the circumstances. The real mistake is to stop trying."

B. F. Skinner

FEBRUARY 28

"That which triggers understanding often is found by bringing misunderstanding to the light."

Dune R. Pascoe

FEBRUARY 29

"I found, as every teacher does, that there is nothing like teaching to help one learn."

Dalai Lama

March

MARCH 1

"True interest appears when the self identifies itself with ideas or objects, when it finds in them a means of expression and they become a necessary form of fuel for its activity."

Jean Piaget

MARCH 2

"Teaching, I soon learned, was a deliberate dance, a constant running conversation, a pleasure."

Siva Vaidhyanathan

MARCH 3

"The teacher should be like the conductor in the orchestra, not the trainer in the circus."

Abhijit Naskar

MARCH 4

"Do not train children to learning by force and harshness, but direct them to it by what amuses their minds."

Plato

MARCH 5

"If a child can't learn the way we teach, maybe we should teach the way they learn."

Ignacio 'Nacho' Estrada

MARCH 6

"A teacher who is attempting to teach without inspiring the pupil with a desire to learn is hammering on cold iron."

Horace Mann

"Sure, they became frustrated with students at times and occasionally displayed impatience, but because they were willing to face the failures of teaching and believed in their capacity to solve problems, they tried not to become defensive with their students or build a wall around themselves. Instead, they tried to take their students seriously as human beings and treated them the way they might treat any colleague, with fairness, compassion, and concern. That approach found reflection in what they taught, how they taught it, and how they evaluated students, but it also appeared in attempts to understand their students' lives, cultures, and aspirations. It even emerged in their willingness to see their students outside of class."

Ken Bain

MARCH 8

"Coverage of material is a snare and a delusion. You begin where students are prepared to begin; and you carry them as far as you can without losing them."

Herbert A. Simon

MARCH 9

" . . . Education is a leading out of what is already there in the pupil's soul."

Muriel Spark

MARCH 10

"There is no such thing a boring content. In the hands of a great teacher . . . even if as teachers we doubt that we can make it so . . . this doubt puts us at risk of undercutting it: watering it down or apologizing for teaching it."

Doug Lemov

MARCH 11

"What the teacher is, is more important than what he teaches."

Karl Menninger

MARCH 12

"A good teacher is one, that never stops listening; a good listener is one, that never stops teaching."

Anthony Liccione

MARCH 13

"When children like a subject, it has something to do with that teacher who taught them to use invisible binoculars in order to look at concepts that are a long way away."

Kavita Bhupta Ghosh

MARCH 14

"A good head and good heart are always a formidable combination. But when you add to that a literate tongue or pen, then you have something very special."

Nelson Mandela

MARCH 15

"The mind grows by self-revelation. In play the child ascertains what he can do, discovers his possibilities of will and thought by exerting his power spontaneously. In work he follows a task prescribed for him by another, and doesn't reveal his own proclivities and inclinations; but another's. In play he reveals his own original power."

Friedrich Froebel

MARCH 16

"Teach them wisely, teach them for life."

Nanette L. Avery

MARCH 17

"Real learning comes about when the competitive spirit has ceased."

Jiddu Krishnamurti

MARCH 18

"The best thing that I can teach you is to be compassionate and kind to all."

Debasish Mridha

MARCH 19

"If you want to build a ship, don't drum up people together to collect wood and don't assign them tasks and work, but rather teach them to long for the endless immensity of the sea."

Antoine de Saint-Exupéry

MARCH 20

"Give a man a teacher and he'll learn many a thing. Teach a man to learn and he'll learn from everything."

Cameron Semmens

MARCH 21

"In teaching you cannot see the fruit of a day's work. It is invisible and remains so, maybe for twenty years."

Jacques Barzun

MARCH 22

"It doesn't matter the materials but what you do and how you interact. Relationships are the most important in the art of teaching. A school can have the most beautiful 'stuff' but it's the care and commitment of a teacher. What matters most is a true teacher with the real stuff inside and helping others discover that real stuff inside themselves."

Jill Telford

MARCH 23

"Without the teacher, there is no teaching."

Lailah Gifty Akita

MARCH 24

"Teaching is not entertainment, but it is unlikely to be successful unless it is entertaining."

Herbert A. Simon

MARCH 25

"During the earliest stages the child perceives things like a solipsist who is unaware of himself as subject and is familiar only with his own actions."

Jean Piage

MARCH 26

"Teaching and learning begins with your heart and brain. Those two things sustain it too."

Jill Telford

MARCH 27

"It is the teacher—what the teacher knows and can do—that is the most significant factor in student achievement."

Harry Wong

MARCH 28

"Education is such a noble profession, it's a
wonderful way to serve."

Erin Gruwell

MARCH 29

"When I walk along with two others, from at least one I will be able to learn."

Confucius

MARCH 30

"Teaching is the most powerful force that changes our world one student at a time."

Debasish Mridha

MARCH 31

"If you want to teach people a new way of thinking, don't bother trying to teach them. Instead, give them a tool, the use of which will lead to new ways of thinking."

Richard Buckminster Fuller

April

APRIL 1

"Half of what you will accomplish in a day will be determined before you leave home. Three quarters of what you achieve will be determined before you enter the classroom door."

Harry Wong

APRIL 2

"Take a minute and think back to your favorite class. Chances are you do not remember the name of the textbook, the name of computer software, or the order in which the curriculum was taught. What you do remember is the person in charge of that class: the teacher."

Oran Tkatchov

APRIL 3

"Never discourage anyone . . . who continually makes progress, no matter how slow."

Plato

APRIL 4

"Just like a seed that needs intensive care to grow into a magnificent tree, a child needs the same amount of love, effort, care, and kindness to grow into a healthy, aware, responsible adult. A sapling doesn't grow with neglect, thirst, or underfeeding, and neither do children. Fulfilling their various needs will help them grow into fine grown-ups who repay kindness with kindness, and return love with love."

Noora Ahmed Alsuwaidi

APRIL 5

"It must be remembered that the purpose of education is not to fill the minds of students with facts . . . it is to teach them to think, if that is possible, and always to think for themselves."

Robert Hutchins

APRIL 6

"To teach is to learn twice over."

Joseph Joubert

APRIL 7

"Every pedagogical situation can be thought of as a kind of triangle among three parties: the student, the teacher, and the world that student and teacher investigate together."

Aaron Hirsh

APRIL 8

"The word 'educate' has as many meanings as there are ideologies in the world and can be interpreted in many ways. One fact, however, is impressive. All those engaged in education agree that education must begin at birth."

Maria Montessori

APRIL 9

"The teachers who get 'burned out' are not the ones who are constantly learning, which can be exhilarating, but those who feel they must stay in control and ahead of the students at all times."

Frank Martin

APRIL 10

"Every student is unique and brings contributions that no one else can make."

Ken Bain

APRIL 11

"If we expect kids to be losers, they will be losers; if we expect them to be winners, they will be winners. They rise, or fall, to the level of the expectations of those around them, especially their parents and their teachers."

Jaime Escalante

APRIL 12

"People's beliefs about their abilities have a profound effect on those abilities."

Albert Bandura

APRIL 13

"Nine-tenths of education is encouragement."

Anatole France

"When you want to teach children to think, you begin by treating them seriously when they are little, giving them responsibilities, talking to them candidly, providing privacy and solitude for them, and making them readers and thinkers of significant thoughts from the beginning. That's if you want to teach them to think."

Bertrand Russell

APRIL 15

"The art of teaching lies in communicating the mystery of the universe without taking the mystery out of it."

Dane R Pascoe

APRIL 16

"Better than a thousand days of diligent study is one day with a great teacher."

Japanese Proverb

APRIL 17

"Good teaching is like a vehicle that runs on four wheels of conceptual efficacy, instinctual guidance, imagination and innovation."

Kavita Bhupta Ghosh

"Good teaching is more a giving of right questions than a giving of right answers."

Josef Albers

" . . . There is a danger of churning out students who are rapid processors of information but may not necessarily be more reflective, thoughtful, and able to give sustained consideration to the information that matters most."

Karen Bohlin

"Encourage effort and praise progress, but be careful that you don't pat mediocre on the back too many times."

T. Jay Taylor

APRIL 21

"[Kids] don't remember what you try to teach them. They remember what you are."

Jim Henson

APRIL 22

"A teacher is never too smart to learn from his pupils."

Bill Bowerman

APRIL 23

"The affects you will have on your students are infinite and currently unknown; you will possibly shape the way they proceed in their careers, the way they will vote, the way they will behave as partners and spouses, the way they will raise their kids."

Donna Quesada

APRIL 24

"It is a mistake to tell students that their classroom is a democracy—it cannot and never will be. But children need to learn how to participate in a community and to prepare themselves for democratic citizenship."

Karen Bohlin

APRIL 25

"No country can really develop unless its citizens are educated."

Nelson Mandela

APRIL 26

"Education is the transmission of civilization."

Will Durant

APRIL 27

"Preaching vs. Teaching: The difference between preaching and teaching: one makes you feel good, the other makes you grow."

T.F. Hodge

APRIL 28

"Teachers are mind engineers! Teachers are life directors! Don't ever undermine a teacher!"

Ernest Agyemang Yeboah

APRIL 29

"As an educator and advocate, I want to be a part of encouraging and supporting movers and shakers of our world. I do not want to be a part of suppressing them."

Jill Telford

APRIL 30

"A classroom is like a greenhouse where the teacher must provide essential amenities like knowledge and life-skill with patience and empathy, control temperatures and provide adequate ventilation to release unwanted energies for everyone and everything to bloom."

Kavita Bhupta Ghosh

MAY 1

"Lessons, however, that enter the soul against its will never grow roots and will never be preserved inside it."

Plato

"Children are like tiny flowers: They are varied and need care, but each is beautiful alone and glorious when seen in the community of peers."

Friedrich Froebel

MAY 3

"Weigh every word that you tell your children, and consider consequence of every action. Children take every word and action seriously. When they think of their childhood, let them remember one kind word, one loving pat and a smile that gave them a million hopes."

Kavita Bhupta Ghosh

MAY 4

"Teaching is the perpetual end and office of all things. Teaching, instruction is the main design that shines through the sky and earth."

Ralph Waldo Emerson

MAY 5

"Education is an ornament in prosperity and a refuge in adversity."

Aristotle

MAY 6

"Everyone who remembers his own education remembers teachers, not methods and techniques. The teacher is the heart of the educational system."

Sidney Hook

MAY 7

"One of the beauties of teaching is that there is no limit to one's growth as a teacher, just as there is no knowing beforehand how much your students can learn."

Herbert Kohl

MAY 8

"The teachers of my life saved my life and sent me out prepared for whatever life I was meant to lead."

Pat Conroy

MAY 9

"If we can recognize what makes us unique, and how we can positively impact our students, then we can make teaching much more meaningful and learning much more rewarding—essentially, a transformative experience for our students."

Carlos Heleno

MAY 10

"I feel a swell of pride. This. This right here is why I wanted to become a teacher. To know that it is possible to change the world for the better..."

Matt Haig

MAY 11

"My heart is singing for joy this morning! A miracle has happened! The light of understanding has shone upon my little pupil's mind, and behold, all things are changed!"

Anne Sullivan Macy

MAY 12

"I didn't care if I wasn't paid for working after school for seven months teaching a 9th grader to read, but when he finally could, priceless! The best times in my life were when I went way beyond my paygrade to service students in need."

Ace Antonio Hall

MAY 13

"What greater joy can a teacher feel than to witness a child's success?"

Michelle L. Graham

MAY 14

"I have no special talent. I am only passionately curious."

Albert Einstein

MAY 15

"No matter what accomplishments you achieve, somebody helped you."

Althea Gibson

MAY 16

"The work of a teacher—exhausting, complex, idiosyncratic, never twice the same—is at its heart an ethical enterprise. Teaching is the vocation of vocations."

William Ayres

MAY 17

"Learn something new, and teach another person something you know. That's how life thrives, progresses and continues. Knowledge is what makes us who we are. The more experience and skills we have and share the better persons we become."

Noora Ahmed Alsuwaidi

MAY 18

"Every great leader is a great teacher, and the greatest leaders seize every opportunity to teach well."

Albert Mohler

MAY 19

"The true teacher defends his pupils against his own personal influence. He inspires self-trust. He guides their eyes from himself to the spirit that quickens him. He will have no disciples."

Amos Bronson Alcott

MAY 20

"The task of the modern educator is not to cut down jungles, but to irrigate deserts."

C. S. Lewis

MAY 21

"The proper education of the young does not consist in stuffing their heads with a mass of words, sentences, and ideas dragged together out of various authors, but in opening up their understanding to the outer world, so that a living stream may flow from their own minds, just as leaves, flowers, and fruit spring from the bud on a tree."

John Amos Comenius

"If you are planning for a year, sow rice; if you are planning for a decade, plant trees; if you are planning for a lifetime, educate people."

Chinese Proverb

"Farmers base their livelihoods on raising crops. But farmers do not make plants grow. They don't attach the roots, glue on the petals, or color the fruit. The plant grows itself. Farmers and gardeners provide the conditions for growth. Good farmers know what those conditions are, and bad ones don't."

Sir Ken Robinson

MAY 24

"Would we rear the human plant to its perfection, we must fertilize the soil which produces it."

Emma Willard

MAY 25

"One looks back with appreciation to the brilliant teachers, but with gratitude to those who touched our human feelings. The curriculum is so much necessary raw material, but warmth is the vital element for the growing plant and for the soul of the child."

Carl Jung

MAY 26

"Students never appreciate their teachers while they are learning. It is only later, when they know more of the world, that they understand how indebted they are to those who instructed them. Good teachers expect no praise or love from the young. They wait for it, and in time, it comes."

Darren Shan

MAY 27

"Teaching means creating situations where structures can be discovered."

Jean Piaget

MAY 28

"The teacher who is indeed wise does not bid you to enter the house of his wisdom but rather leads you to the threshold of your mind."

Khalil Gibran

MAY 29

"What all good teachers have in common, however, is that they set high standards for their students and do not settle for anything less."

Marva Collins

MAY 30

"The teacher's happy task is to show them the path to perfection, furnishing the means and removing the obstacles, beginning with those which she herself is likely to present (for the teacher can be the greatest obstacle of all). If discipline had already arrived our work would hardly be needed; the child's instinct would be a safe enough guide enabling him to deal with every difficulty."

Maria Montessori

"Teaching is a creative profession, it is our duty as school leaders and education influencers to offer the right climate to foster innovation and support innovative teaching practices within our schools, and that's what will make our students succeed in the 21st century."

Samer Chidiac

June

JUNE 1

"It is the supreme art of the teacher to awaken joy in creative expression and knowledge."

Albert Einstein

JUNE 2

"What sculpture is to a block of marble,
education is to a human soul."

Joseph Addison

JUNE 3

"Teachers should not fear going off plan if a better learning opportunity presents itself. Plans are plans, but children are living, breathing, creative people, who deserve to have their questions answered and original ideas explored."

Adele Devine

JUNE 4

"I have come to believe that a great teacher
is a great artist and that there are as few
as there are any other great artists. It might
even be the greatest of the arts since the
medium is the human mind and spirit."

John Steinbeck

JUNE 5

"A good teacher is like a good artist. They go right to the most difficult part of whatever's going on."

Bruce Nauman

JUNE 6

"The art of teaching is the art of assisting discovery."

Mark Van Doren

JUNE 7

"Play is the highest expression of human development in childhood for it alone is the free expression of what is in a child's soul."

Friedrich Froebel

JUNE 8

"The best teaching is often both an intellectual creation and a performing art."

Ken Bain

JUNE 9

"The teacher's task is to initiate the learning process and then get out of the way."

John Warren

JUNE 10

"When we think about learning, we typically focus on getting information into students' heads. What if, instead, we focus on getting information out of students' heads?"

Pooja K. Agarwal

JUNE 11

"The teacher is of course an artist, but being an artist does not mean that he or she can make the profile, can shape the students. What an educator does in teaching is to make it possible for the students to become themselves."

Paulo Freire

JUNE 12

"To this end, the greatest asset of a school is the personality of the teacher."

John Strachan

JUNE 13

"Benevolence alone will not make a teacher, nor will learning alone do it. The gift of teaching is a peculiar talent, and implies a need and a craving in the teacher himself."

John Jay Chapman

"When the untapped potential of a student meets the liberating art of a teacher, a miracle unfolds."

Mary Hatwood Futrell

JUNE 15

"No matter what your circumstance, if you provide kids with creative ammunition, they will blast holes into an oppressive reality, and conceive limitless worlds."

A. J. Mendez Brooks

JUNE 16

"Wherever you find something extraordinary, you'll find the fingerprints of a great teacher."

Arne Duncan

JUNE 17

"An effective educator who can embrace the ever-changing teaching and learning environment, maintain resilience and strength under this pressure, dynamically participate in the development of new practices, and continue to foster a love of learning stands a greater chance of captivating students and appealing to their needs."

Carlos Heleno

JUNE 18

"Effective teaching may be the hardest job
there is."

William Glasser

JUNE 19

"There are two types of teachers. The ones who teach you to use the text to find answers, and the ones who teach you to use the text to find another whole world of answers."

Anonymous

JUNE 20

"Teaching is a dialogue, and it is through the process of engaging students that we see ideas taken from the abstract and played out in concrete visual form. Students teach us about creativity through their personal responses."

Martha Boles

JUNE 21

"We need to help students and parents cherish and preserve the ethnic and cultural diversity that nourishes and strengthens this community—and this nation."

Cesar Chavez

"I have an historical, a cultural, and a moral obligation to give back something to my country. So, I became a teacher."

Vartan Gregorian

JUNE 23

"Education is the great engine of personal development. It is through education that the daughter of a peasant can become a doctor, that the son of a mine worker can become the head of the mine, that a child of farm workers can become the president of a great nation. It is what we make out of what we have, not what we are given, that separates one person from another."

Nelson Mandela

JUNE 24

"We cannot educate the citizens of
tomorrow based on the requirements of
yesterday."

Abhijit Naskar

JUNE 25

"What greater or better gift can we offer the republic than to teach and instruct our youth?"

Cicero

JUNE 26

"All who have meditated on the art of governing mankind have been convinced that the fate of empires depends on the education of youth."

Aristotle

JUNE 27

"Teaching career does not begin with the completion of graduation and post-graduation and attaining a degree—it begins the moment one starts caring about learners."

Kavita Bhupta Ghosh

JUNE 28

"The best teaching can be done only when there is a direct individual relationship between a student and a good teacher—a situation in which the student discusses the ideas, thinks about the things, and talks about the things. It's impossible to learn very much by simply sitting in a lecture, or even by simply doing problems that are assigned."

Richard Feynman

JUNE 29

"When you teach, you learn."

Meir Ezra

JUNE 30

"Teaching kids to count is fine, but teaching them what counts is best."

Bob Talbert

July

JULY 1

"True teachers are those who use themselves as bridges over which they invite their students to cross; then, having facilitated their crossing, joyfully collapse, encouraging them to create their own."

Nikos Kazantzakis

JULY 2

"Do not confine your children to your own
learning, for they were born in another time."

Chinese Proverb

JULY 3

"Pedagogy must be oriented not to the yesterday, but to the tomorrow of the child's development. Only then can it call to life in the process of education those processes of development which now lie in the zone of proximal development."

Lev S. Vygotsky

"Young children who constantly hear "person" praise ("you're so smart to do this well") as opposed to "task" praise ("you did that well") are more likely to believe that intelligence is fixed rather than expandable with hard work."

Ken Bain

JULY 5

"The most successful classes are those where the teacher has a clear idea of what is expected from the students and the students know what the teacher expects from them."

Harry Wong

JULY 6

"You cannot teach a man anything, you can only help him find it within himself."

Galileo

JULY 7

"If you want your children to be smart and wise, then teach them to think and not to memorize."

Mouloud Benzadi

JULY 8

"Education is not the filling of a pot but the lighting of a fire."

W.B. Yeats

JULY 9

"The object of education is to prepare the young to educate themselves throughout their lives."

Robert Hutchins

JULY 10

"The best teachers are those who show you where to look, but don't tell you what to see."

Alexandra K. Trenfor

JULY 11

"I am not a teacher, but an awakener."

Robert Frost

JULY 12

"Teachers can change lives with just the right mix of chalk and challenges."

Joyce Meyer

JULY 13

"The mediocre teacher tells. The good teacher explains. The superior teacher demonstrates. The great teacher inspires."

William Arthur Ward

JULY 14

"All students can learn and succeed, but not in the same way and not in the same day."

William G. Spady

JULY 15

"The only way you can teach is by validation."

Meir Ezra

JULY 16

"Teaching holds a mirror to the soul. If I am willing to look in that mirror and not run from what I see I have a chance to gain self-knowledge and knowing myself is as crucial to good teaching as knowing my students and my subject. In fact, knowing my students and my subject depends heavily on self-knowledge."

Parker J. Palmer

JULY 17

"Education is much more than a matter of imparting the knowledge and skills by which narrow goals are achieved. It is also about opening the child's eyes to the needs and rights of others."

Dalai Lama

JULY 18

"Once children learn how to learn, nothing is going to narrow their mind. The essence of teaching is to make learning contagious, to have one idea spark another."

Marva Collins

JULY 19

"A teacher is only as effective as his ability to understand where his student is."

Abraham Hicks

JULY 20

"Education is a painful, continual, and difficult work to be done in kindness, by watching, by warning, by praise, but above all, by example."

John Ruskin

JULY 21

"Meaningful student involvement is the process of engaging students as partners in every facet of school change for the purpose strengthening their commitment to education, community & democracy."

Adam Fletcher

JULY 22

"The task for parents and teachers is not to teach, it is how to inspire the people of youth to find their desire to learn."

Hasse Jerner

JULY 23

"Educators are spiritual beings—we are on earth to make a difference."

Holly Elissa Bruno

JULY 24

"Children have real understanding only of that which they invent themselves, and each time that we try to teach them too quickly, we keep them from reinventing it themselves."

Jean Piaget

JULY 25

"The only real ill-doing is the deprivation of knowledge."

Plato

JULY 26

"The true direction of the development of thinking is not from the individual to the social, but from the social to the individual."

Lev S. Vygotsky

JULY 27

"High quality programs require and foster a norm of continuous teaching improvement."

Swen Nater

JULY 28

"I have always felt that the true text-book for the pupil is his teacher."

Mahatma Gandhi

JULY 29

"Woe to him who teaches men faster than they can learn."

Will Durant

"Understanding a question is half an answer."

Socrates

JULY 31

"I want students to engage the way a clutch on a car gets engaged: an engine can be running, making appropriate noises, burning fuel and creating exhaust fumes, but unless the clutch is engaged, nothing moves. It's all sound and smoke, and nobody gets anywhere."

Robert L. Fried

August

AUGUST 1

"A good teacher is not one who never doubts, but rather one who strives to keep on learning despite the doubts in her mind."

Nahoko Uehashi

AUGUST 2

"One child, one teacher, one book, one pen can change the world."

Malala Yousafzai

AUGUST 3

"A well-managed classroom is a task-oriented and predictable environment."

Harry Wong

AUGUST 4

"Each time I walk into a classroom, I can choose the place within myself from which my teaching will come, just as I can choose the place within my students toward which my teaching will be aimed. I need not teach from a fearful place: I can teach from my curiosity or hope or empathy or honesty, places that are as real within me as are my fears. I can have fear, but I need not be fear—if I am willing to stand somewhere else in my inner landscape."

Parker J. Palmer

AUGUST 5

"What we want is to see the child in pursuit of knowledge, and not knowledge in pursuit of the child."

George Bernard Shaw

AUGUST 6

"It is a greater work to educate a child, in the true and larger sense of the word, than to rule a state."

Dr. William Ellery Channing

AUGUST 7

"You can teach a student a lesson for a day, but if you can teach him to learn by creating curiosity, he will continue the learning process as long as he lives."

Clay P. Bedford

AUGUST 8

"Education's purpose is to replace an empty
mind with an open one."

Malcolm Forbes

AUGUST 9

"Praise is essential in developing the right attitude toward learning and toward school."

Marva Collins

AUGUST 10

"Good teaching is one-fourth preparation
and three-fourths theatre."

Gail Goldwin

AUGUST 11

"Ask 'How will they learn best?' not 'Can they learn?'."

Jaime Escalante

AUGUST 12

"I have learned that, although I am a good teacher, I am a much better student, and I was blessed to learn valuable lessons from my students on a daily basis. They taught me the importance of teaching to a student— and not to a test."

Erin Gruwell

AUGUST 13

"Proper teaching is recognized with ease. You can know it without fail because it awakens within you that sensation which tells you this is something you have always known."

Frank Herbert

AUGUST 14

"It's the teacher that makes the difference,
not the classroom."

Michael Morpurgo

AUGUST 15

"The most important day of a person's education is the first day of school, not Graduation Day."

Harry Wong

"The most important function of education at any level is to develop the personality of the individual and the significance of his life to himself and to others. This is the basic architecture of a life; the rest is ornamentation and decoration of the structure."

Grayson Kirk

AUGUST 17

"What we instill in our children will be the foundation upon which they build their future."

Steve Maraboli

AUGUST 18

"At its highest level, the purpose of teaching is not to teach—it is to inspire the desire for learning. Once a student's mind is set on fire, it will find a way to provide its own fuel."

Sydney . I. Harris

AUGUST 19

"A great teacher is like a fountain; she draws from the still, deep waters of personal growth and professional knowledge to serve others from her abundant overflow."

Wynn Godbold

AUGUST 20

"When someone is taught the joy of learning, it becomes a life-long process that never stops, a process that creates a logical individual. That is the challenge and joy of teaching."

Marva Collins

AUGUST 21

"The whole purpose of education is to turn mirrors into windows."

Sydney J. Harris

AUGUST 22

"The future of the world is in my classroom today, a future with the potential for good or bad . . . Several future presidents are learning from me today; so are the great writers of the next decades, and so are all the so-called ordinary people who will make the decisions in a democracy."

Ivan Welton Fitzwater

AUGUST 23

"Education is the realization of hope for the future."

Victor Tam

AUGUST 24

"A teacher affects eternity; he can never tell where his influence stops."

Henry B. Adams

"The most difficult thing, as teachers know, is not to move. It is more difficult not to move than to move well; for this reason, children must have much practice in moving well and in controlling their motions before exercising the will to successfully inhibit every voluntary movement."

Maria Montessori

AUGUST 26

"He is not necessarily the best teacher who performs the most labour; makes his pupils work the hardest, and bustle the most. A hundred cents of copper, though they make more clatter and fill more space, have only a tenth of the value of one gold eagle."

Emma Willard

AUGUST 27

"I like a teacher who gives you something to take home to think about besides homework."

Lily Tomlin

AUGUST 28

"Teaching mathematics, like teaching any art, requires the ability to inspire the student. Inspiration requires marketing, and marketing requires stirring communication."

Hartosh Singh Bal

AUGUST 29

"To learn a thing in life and through doing is much more developing, cultivating, and strengthening than to learn it merely through the verbal communication of ideas."

Friedrich Froebel

AUGUST 30

"The difference between a beginning teacher and an experienced one is that the beginning teacher asks, 'How am I doing?' and the experienced teacher asks, 'How are the children doing?'."

Esmé Raji Codell

AUGUST 31

"Good teaching must be slow enough so that it is not confusing, and fast enough so that it is not boring."

Sydney J. Harris

September

SEPTEMBER 1

"The greatest challenge a teacher has to accept is the courage to be; if we *are*, we make mistakes; we say too much where we should have said nothing; we do not speak where a word might have made all the difference. If we are, we will make terrible errors. But we still have to have the courage to struggle on, trusting in our own points of reference to show us the way."

Madeleine L. Engle

SEPTEMBER 2

"Education begins at the level of the learner."

Aristotle

SEPTEMBER 3

"The test of a good teacher is not how many questions he can ask his pupils that they will answer readily, but how many questions he inspires them to ask him which he finds it hard to answer."

Alice Wellington Rollins

SEPTEMBER 4

"Children must be taught how to think, not what to think."

Margaret Mead

SEPTEMBER 5

"The purpose of education should be to nourish and strengthen a student's capacity, not to force-feed all students the same material . . . "

Abhijit Naskar

SEPTEMBER 6

"The best education is not given to students;
it is drawn out of them."

Gerald Belcher

SEPTEMBER 7

"I cannot teach anybody anything; I can only make them think."

Socrates

SEPTEMBER 8

"Spoon feeding in the long run teaches us nothing but the shape of the spoon."

E. M. Forster

SEPTEMBER 9

"There are two kinds of teachers: the kind that fill you with so much quail shot that you can't move, and the kind that just gives you a little prod behind and you jump to the skies."

Robert Frost

SEPTEMBER 10

"The greatest sign of success for a teacher . . . is to be able to say, 'The children are now working as if I did not exist'."

Maria Montessori

SEPTEMBER 11

"Everything should be made as simple as possible, but not simpler."

Albert Einstein

"Successful instruction is constant, rigorous, integrated across disciplines, connected to students' lived cultures, connected to their intellectual legacies, engaging, and designed for problem solving that is useful beyond the classroom."

Lisa Delpit

SEPTEMBER 13

"An error means a child needs help, not a reprimand or ridicule for doing something wrong."

Marva Collins

SEPTEMBER 14

"Bright and well-behaved students can be taught anywhere and by anyone, but real success is when a teacher is able to engage the naughtiest and the least interested student unconditionally in the classroom."

Kavita Bhupta Ghosh

SEPTEMBER 15

"Never send negligent pupils out of the classroom. Be patient with their light-mindedness."

John Bosco

SEPTEMBER 16

"Real education happens only by failing, changing, challenging, and adjusting. All of those gerunds apply to teachers as well as students. No person is an 'educator,' because education is not something one person does to another. Education is an imprecise process, a dance, and a collaborative experience."

Siva Vaidhyanathan

SEPTEMBER 17

"The single greatest effect on student achievement is not race, it is not poverty—it is the effectiveness of the teacher."

Harry Wong

SEPTEMBER 18

"Teach the way you'd want to be taught."

Anonymous

SEPTEMBER 19

"Remember that failure is an event, not a person."

Zig Ziglar

SEPTEMBER 20

"If you get hurt every time someone misunderstands or demonstrates their unwillingness to learn, you'll never build the experience needed to get truly good at teaching and, therefore, will never experience the rewards of doing it well."

Anthony J. Stieber

SEPTEMBER 21

"So much of teaching is sharing. Learning results in sharing, sharing results in change, change is learning. The only other job with so much sharing is parenting. That's probably why the two are so often confused."

Esmé Raji Codell

SEPTEMBER 22

"You teach me, I forget. You show me, I remember. You involve me, I understand."

Edward O. Wilson

SEPTEMBER 23

"Education is what survives when what has been learned has been forgotten."

B. F. Skinner

SEPTEMBER 24

"What a child can do today with assistance,
she will be able to do by herself tomorrow."

Lev S. Vygotsky

SEPTEMBER 25

"The direction in which education starts a man will determine his future life."

Plato

SEPTEMBER 26

"I am indebted to my father for living, but to my teacher for living well."

Alexander the Great

SEPTEMBER 27

"Teaching requires that you work at being a person and work at understanding people and the world, and work at feelings and connecting and respect in ways and to a magnitude that is not often asked of adults."

Tom Rademacher

SEPTEMBER 28

"It is not enough to simply listen to student voice. Educators have an ethical imperative to do something with students, and that is why meaningful student involvement is vital to school improvement."

Adam Fletcher

SEPTEMBER 29

"Education and admonition commence in the first years if childhood, and last to the very end of life."

Plato

SEPTEMBER 30

"We are all concerned about the future of American education. But as I tell my students, you do not enter the future—you create the future. The future is created through hard work."

Jaime Escalante

October

OCTOBER 1

"I think the teaching profession contributes more to the future of our society than any other single profession."

John Wooden

OCTOBER 2

"The ability to think straight, some knowledge of the past, some vision of the future, some skill to do useful service, some urge to fit that service into the well-being of the community—these are the most vital things education must try to produce."

Virginia Gildersleeve

OCTOBER 3

"Teaching is the greatest act of optimism."

Colleen Wilcox

OCTOBER 4

"The most important part of teaching is to teach what it is to know."

Simone Weil

OCTOBER 5

"The dream begins, most of the time, with a teacher who believes in you, who tugs and pushes and leads you on to the next plateau, sometimes poking you with a sharp stick called truth."

Dan Rather

OCTOBER 6

"Teaching is truth mediated by personality."

Phyllis Brooks

OCTOBER 7

"Instead of dictating to them 'who' and 'what' they should be. Be a good role model. Teach them well. Allow them to be true to who they are and encourage them to be their 'authentic self.'"

Sepideh Irvani

OCTOBER 8

"Isn't the point of education to teach students how to think, not what to think?"

Lindsey Whittington

OCTOBER 9

"Teach them the quiet words of kindness, to live beyond themselves. Urge them toward excellence, drive them toward gentleness, pull them deep into yourself, pull them upward toward manhood, but softly like an angel arranging clouds. Let your spirit move through them softly."

Pat Conroy

OCTOBER 10

"Children require guidance and sympathy far more than instruction."

Anne Sullivan Macy

OCTOBER 11

"Every child deserves a champion—an adult who will never give up on them, who understands the power of connection and insists that they become the best that they can possibly be."

Rita Pierson

OCTOBER 12

"Most of us end up with no more than five or six people who remember us. Teachers have thousands of people who remember them for the rest of their lives."

Andy Rooney

OCTOBER 13

"Teaching is the art of serendipity. Each of us has the experience of finding out that something we intended as only the most casual of remarks, or the stray example, changes the way some students thought to the point of changing their lives."

Gregory C. Carlson

OCTOBER 14

"I'm not a teacher: only a fellow traveler of whom you asked the way. I pointed ahead—ahead of myself as well as you."

George Bernard Shaw

OCTOBER 15

"Instruction is good for a child; but example is worth more."

Alexandre Dumas

OCTOBER 16

"Are we forming children who are only capable of learning what is already known? Or should we try to develop creative and innovative minds, capable of discovery from the preschool age on, throughout life?"

Jean Piaget

OCTOBER 17

"The single problem plaguing all students in all schools everywhere is the crisis of disconnection. Meaningful Student Involvement happens when the roles of students are actively re-aligned from being the passive recipients of schools to becoming active partners throughout the educational process."

Adam Fletcher

OCTOBER 18

"I believe that education is the greatest equalizer; thus, I will continue to fight to equalize the playing field in an educational atmosphere that is not always level!"

Erin Gruwell

OCTOBER 19

"At the desk where I sit, I have learned one great truth. The answer for all our national problems—the answer for all the problems of the world—comes to a single word. That word is education."

Lyndon B. Johnson

OCTOBER 20

"Knowledge is the eye of the desire and can become the pilot of the soul."

Will Durant

OCTOBER 21

"The important thing is not so much that every child should be taught as that every child should be given the wish to learn."

John Lubbock

OCTOBER 22

"The educated differ from the uneducated
as much as the living differ from the dead."

Aristotle

OCTOBER 23

"Intelligence is what you use when you don't know what to do."

Jean Piaget

OCTOBER 24

"When one teaches, two learn."

Robert Heinlein

OCTOBER 25

"The only 'good' learning is that which is in advance of development."

Lev S. Vygotsky

OCTOBER 26

"One of the greatest gifts a caring teacher can contribute to children is to help them learn to sit when they feel like running, to raise their hand when they feel like talking, to be polite to their neighbor, to stand in line without pushing, and to do their homework when they feel like playing. By introducing procedures in the classroom, you are also introducing procedures as a way of living a happy and successful life."

Harry Wong

OCTOBER 27

"I am a teacher born and bred, and I believe in the advocacy of teachers. It's a calling. We want our students to feel impassioned and empowered."

Erin Gruwell

OCTOBER 28

"Real education changes you on the inside."

Edward Mooney, Jr.

OCTOBER 29

"I am thankful and blessed to be in a position where I have learned as much from those that have taught me as I have from those that I continue to teach."

Kim Ha Campbell

OCTOBER 30

"We never know which lives we influence, or when, or why."

Stephen King

OCTOBER 31

"We must trust that what we're doing has a purpose. We must realize that we're not here to make kids conform or perform, but that we're here to help them to develop their own unique skills and talents, not the ones we want them to have or the ones we think they should have."

Tom Walsh

November

NOVEMBER 1

"The master said, 'A true teacher is one who, keeping the past alive, is also able to understand the present'."

Confucius

NOVEMBER 2

"The principal goal of education in the schools should be creating men and women who are capable of doing new things, not simply repeating what other generations have done."

Jean Piaget

NOVEMBER 3

"If we teach today's students as we taught yesterday's, we rob them of tomorrow."

John Dewey

NOVEMBER 4

"I teach not by feeding the mind with data
but by kindling the mind."

Debasish Mridha

NOVEMBER 5

"Everyday more educators are showing that they value students by involving them in meaningful ways in school. These teachers and administrators say that it is not about 'making students happy' or allowing students to run the school. Their experience shows that when educators partner with students to improve learning, teaching and leadership in schools, school change is positive and effective."

Adam Fletcher

NOVEMBER 6

"If we spark a student's passion, we unleash a powerful force upon the world."

Tim Fargo

NOVEMBER 7

"Experienced campers know that you need to put more wood on the fire to keep it going. Experienced leaders know that the fires of enthusiasm can't continue without regular and consistent action."

Reed B. Markham

NOVEMBER 8

"Education is the kindling of a flame, not the filling of a vessel."

Socrates

NOVEMBER 9

"Do not give them a candle to light the way, teach them how to make fire instead. That is the meaning of enlightenment."

Kamand Kojouri

NOVEMBER 10

"You haven't made a fire till it has burned.
You haven't made a dollar till it's earned.
And no teaching has transpired If the child
has not acquired. You haven't taught a child
till he has learned."

Swen Nater

NOVEMBER 11

"Teachers see coldness in the world and light fires in the minds of their students, hoping for a warm summer."

Lance Conrad

NOVEMBER 12

"Like the sun, a teacher enlightens a mind
with his love, warmth, and light."

Debasish Mridha

NOVEMBER 13

"A good teacher is like a candle—it consumes itself to light the way for others."

Mustafa Kemal Atatürk

NOVEMBER 14

"Education in the light of present-day knowledge and need calls for some spirited and creative innovations both in the substance and the purpose of current pedagogy."

Anne Sullivan Macy

NOVEMBER 15

"If a man is to shed the light of the sun upon other men, he must first of all have it within himself."

Romain Rolland

NOVEMBER 16

"Education is not to reform students or amuse them or to make them expert technicians. It is to unsettle their minds, widen their horizons, inflame their intellects, teach them to think straight, if possible."

Robert Hutchins

NOVEMBER 17

"Gift last for few days, guidance last forever."

Amit Kalantri

NOVEMBER 18

"A good teacher isn't someone who gives the answers out to their kids but is understanding of needs and challenges and gives tools to help other people succeed."

Justin Trudeau

NOVEMBER 19

"The teacher must adopt the role of facilitator not content provider."

Lev S. Vygotsky

NOVEMBER 20

"Those who educate children well are more to be honored than they who produce them; for these only gave them life, those the art of living well."

Aristotle

NOVEMBER 21

"I never teach my pupils; I only attempt to provide the conditions in which they can learn."

Albert Einstein

NOVEMBER 22

"In an effective classroom, students should not only know what they are doing, they should also know why and how."

Harry Wong

NOVEMBER 23

"Don't try to fix the students, fix ourselves first. The good teacher makes the poor student good and the good student superior. When our students fail, we, as teachers, too, have failed."

Marva Collins

NOVEMBER 24

"If kids come to educators and teachers from strong, healthy, functioning families, it makes our job easier. If they do not come to us from strong, healthy, functioning families, it makes our job more important."

Barbara Coloroso

NOVEMBER 25

"Education is not preparation for life; education is life itself."

John Dewey

NOVEMBER 26

"To benefit from what the best teachers do, however, we must embrace a different model, one in which teaching occurs only when learning takes place. Most fundamentally, teaching in this conception is creating those conditions in which most—if not all—of our students will realize their potential to learn. That sounds like hard work, and it is a little scary because we don't have complete control over who we are, but it is highly rewarding and obtainable."

Ken Bain

NOVEMBER 27

"In a completely rational society, the best of us would be teachers and the rest of us would have to settle for something less."

Lee Iacocca

NOVEMBER 28

"A good teacher does something more than teaching; he makes you start learning."

Raheel Farooq

NOVEMBER 29

"If a man neglects education, he walks lame to the end of his life."

Plato

NOVEMBER 30

"The whole art of teaching is only the art of awakening the natural curiosity of the mind for the purpose of satisfying it afterwards."

Anatole France

December

DECEMBER 1

"To me the sole hope of human salvation lies in teaching."

George Bernard Shaw

DECEMBER 2

"Whatever you teach your children will be mirrored reflection of you in everything they are and in everything they do However which way you treat your children will follow you to the grave so teach them to be just and noble teach them to be strong and brave."

Richard Fleming

DECEMBER 3

"Teachers believe they have a gift for giving; it drives them with the same irrepressible drive that drives others to create a work of art or a market or a building."

A. Bartlett Giamatti

DECEMBER 4

"Great teachers share more than the facts,
they share values."

Reed B. Markham

DECEMBER 5

"I'll always choose a teacher with enthusiasm and weak technique over one with brilliant strategies but who is just punching the clock. Why? An enthusiastic teacher can learn technique, but it is almost impossible to light a fire inside the charred heart of a burned-out teacher."

Dave Burgess

DECEMBER 6

"Good teachers know how to bring out the best in students."

Charles Kuralt

DECEMBER 7

"For good nurture and education implant good constitutions."

Plato

"If you treat every question like you've never heard it before, your students feel like you respect them, and everyone learns a lot more. Including the teacher."

Anita Diamant

DECEMBER 9

"Wonder is the beginning of wisdom."

Socrates

DECEMBER 10

"In all of my teaching, I think about what I find fascinating and what I would love to learn more about. I use my teaching to grow, and that makes me, even after all these years, a fresh and eager teacher."

Carol S. Dweck

DECEMBER 11

"The average teacher explains complexity; the gifted teacher reveals simplicity."

Robert Brault

DECEMBER 12

"The greatest gift we can give our children is teaching them accountability."

Ron Baratono

DECEMBER 13

"If someone is going down the wrong road, he doesn't need motivation to speed him up. What he needs is education to turn him around."

Jim Rohn

DECEMBER 14

"People not only gain understanding through reflection, they evaluate and alter their own thinking."

Albert Bandura

DECEMBER 15

"Give instruction to a wise man, and he will be still wiser; teach a righteous man, and he will increase in learning."

Proverbs 9:9

DECEMBER 16

"You can teach a person all you know, but only experience will convince him that what you say is true."

Richelle E. Goodrich

DECEMBER 17

"Teaching should be such that what is offered is perceived as a valuable gift and not as a hard duty."

Albert Einstein

DECEMBER 18

"I entered the classroom with the conviction that it was crucial for me and every other student to be an active participant, not a passive consumer . . . education that connects the will to know with the will to become."

Bell Hooks

DECEMBER 19

"A good teacher can inspire hope, ignite the imagination, and instill a love of learning."

Brad Henry

DECEMBER 20

"Let the main object . . . to seek and to find a method of instruction, by which teachers may teach less, but learners learn more."

John Amos Comenius

DECEMBER 21

"Education, for most people, means trying to lead the child to resemble the typical adult of his society . . . but for me and no one else, education means making creators. . . You have to make inventors, innovators . . . not conformists."

Jean Piaget

DECEMBER 22

"You can't really teach a kid anything: you can only show him the way and motivate him to learn it himself."

Dave Cullen

DECEMBER 23

"The job of an educator is to teach students to see vitality in themselves."

Joseph Campbell

DECEMBER 24

"By giving our students practice in talking with others, we give them frames for thinking on their own."

Lev S. Vygotsky

DECEMBER 25

"Do to others whatever you would like them to do to you. This is the essence of all that is taught in the law and the prophets."

Jesus of Nazareth

DECEMBER 26

"There is no nobler profession, nor no greater calling, than to be among those unheralded many who gave and give their lives to the preservation of human knowledge, passed with commitment and care from one generation to the next."

Laurence Overmire

DECEMBER 27

"Three things give the student the possibility of surpassing his teacher: ask a lot of questions, remember the answers, teach."

John Amos Comenius

DECEMBER 28

"The moments of the class must belong to the student—not the students, but to the very undivided student. You don't teach a class. You teach a student."

Ken Bain

DECEMBER 29

"Experience precedes understanding."

Jean Piaget

DECEMBER 30

"Just like the sacrifice of parenting, teaching is a daily 'giving away' of myself. I give my time and my energy, my knowledge and my care. I give stories and I give listening. I give my attention and my interest. I give of myself. I give myself away. And I do it because I love it—because I love seeing children grow and learn and develop. I invest in my students, letting them know that I see them, that I believe they can learn, that I value their efforts . . . That they are important to me. And I do this, this giving and investing, because I know that the best kind of teaching stems from an authentic relationship. Don't tell them what you know until you show them that you care."

Gabbie Stroud

DECEMBER 31

"Students don't care how much you know until they know how much you care."

Anonymous

a matthew kelly company

FLOYD

we grow people.

"It is easy to get so caught up in surviving
that we stop dreaming."

Matthew Kelly

. . . .

WHAT ARE YOUR DREAMS FOR YOUR LIFE?
WHAT ARE YOUR DREAMS FOR
YOUR SCHOOL?

Floyd's *Bigger and Better Future for Schools* training
experience provides educators with the same tools
utilized by top companies across the country to
empower them to pursue their dreams and become
the-best-version-of themselves.

Discover what this powerful program can do
for you and your school.

www.BBF4Schools.com
info@floydconsulting.com I 866-499-2049

A BIGGER *better* FUTURE

GREAT LEADERSHIP STARTS WITH

Yourself.

INSIGHT FROM FAMOUS LEADERS
TO KEEP YOU INSPIRED 365 DAYS A YEAR

Leaders Inspiring Leaders

New York Times Bestselling Author
MATTHEW KELLY